Gover
Rea

NoLexil B

THE
MOUNTAIN
MEN

THE
MOUNTAIN
MEN

BY JAMES L. COLLINS

Franklin Watts
A Division of Grolier Publishing

New York London Hong Kong Sydney
Danbury, Connecticut

Cover photograph copyright ©: North Wind Picture Archives
Photographs copyright ©: North Wind Picture Archives: frontis, pp. 15 (inset), 16,
20, 24, 30, 37 (both); Wyoming Division of Tourism: pp. 11 (Jeff Olson), 28 34;
The Bettmann Archive: pp. 8, 15 top, 16 (inset), 33, 56; St. Louis Mercantile
Library: pp. 12, 18, 22, 42, 46, 50 54; Missouri Historical Society: p. 21; New York
Public Library, Schomburg Collection: p. 38; NewYork Public Library, Picture Col-
lection: p. 52.

Library of Congress Cataloging-in-Publication Data

Collins, James L., 1945-
The mountain men / by James L. Collins.
p. cm. — (A First book)
Includes bibliographical references (p.) and index.
ISBN 0-531-20229-1
1. West (U.S.)—History—To 1848—Biography—Juvenile literature.
2. West (U.S.)—History—1848-1860—Biography—Juvenile literature.
3. Fur traders—West (U.S.)—Biography—Juvenile literature.
4. Trappers—West (U.S.)—Biography—Juvenile literature.
5. Explorers—West (U.S.)—Biography—Juvenile literature.
I. Title. II. Series.
F592.C68 1996
978'.02'0922—dc20
95-49301 CIP
[B]

Contents

Introduction

To us, the mountain areas of the West—the Rockies, the Sierra Nevada, and the Cascades—remain sanctuaries of true wilderness, the only regions of the United States not manicured by European cultivation.

Compared to the West of the early nineteenth century, however, these mountains are now tame.

Traveling west across the Great Plains and Rockies in the days of the mountain men was akin to walking off the edge of the earth, and in many ways these travelers were the astronauts of their day. Thriving on the opportunity to explore the unknown, they charted remote lands that the nation hoped to inhabit someday.

Who were the mountain men? They were not just explorers who after trekking through the West returned to their comfortable homes to digest the data they had collected. A mountain man made the mountains his home. He was more than an explorer; he was an inventor, an entrepreneur, a diplomat, a ranger, a warrior, a survivor, and a storyteller. These are the stories of their lives.

Following the 1803 Louisiana Purchase, which doubled the size of the United States, explorers Meriwether Lewis and William Clark were dispatched to chart the newly acquired territory.

CHAPTER I
JOHN COLTER
(1775 – 1813)

Although John Colter was said to be the original mountain man, he lived in obscurity until 1803, when he joined Lewis and Clark on their voyage of discovery. A hunter for the expedition, he came across a wide variety of animals seldom seen on the eastern seaboard as Lewis and Clark neared the mouth of the Columbia River on the Pacific coast. Among these animals was an enormous amount of beaver, sighted mostly in the Rocky Mountain region, which were valued for their fur. It's no wonder, then, that on the trip back home, John Colter asked Lewis and Clark if he could be discharged from his duties early. Two hunters, named Dixon and Potts, had persuaded him to return to the mountains he had just come from so he could trap the abundant beaver.

This decision marked the beginning of Colter's life as a man who would spend nearly all of his time in the mountains trapping beaver. John Colter had become a mountain man.

After leaving Lewis and Clark, Colter spent the entire winter wandering about the region now known as the Rocky Mountains, probably in the area that today is Yellowstone National Park. On his way to St. Louis the following spring (1807), he encountered an expedition of trappers led by Manuel Lisa, a Spaniard who would be just as well known as Colter in the annals of the fur trade. Once again Colter was persuaded to head back to the Rocky Mountains, where he served as a guide for Lisa.

Colter was sent ahead to inform the local tribes that Lisa and his men had arrived to trade furs. It turned out to be a fateful trip, for from that time on, the white man was seen as an intruder into the mountains—at least for one tribe. While the details are sketchy, the fact remains that two Blackfoot Indians were killed by

Many of John Colter's discoveries were first beheld in what is today Yellowstone National Park in Wyoming.

men from the Lewis and Clark expedition as they returned to St. Louis in 1806. Prior to this, the Blackfeet had been very peaceful toward the white man, as were nearly all of the Indian tribes encountered by Lewis and Clark. But the Blackfeet, after losing two men, became suspicious when a white man came into view, for they did not know what his true intentions were. The Crow Indians, on the other hand, got along quite well with the white man, and with John Colter in particular. Colter had been visiting the Crow when the tribe was attacked by its mortal enemy, the Blackfeet. Colter fought alongside the Crow and received an arrow in his leg. But he was spotted by the Blackfeet, and this further inflamed their hostility toward white men who might wander into their territory.

Men like John Colter were just as much explorers as they were fur trappers. In fact, Colter is recorded in history as being the first white man to do a number of things. For example, he was the first white man to explore the Big Horn River. He was the first white explorer to cross the passes at the head of the Wind

This etching illustrates John Colter's flight from the Blackfoot Indians. He barely escaped.

River and see the headwaters of the Colorado River. He was the first to see the Teton Mountains, and what would become known as Jackson Hole and Pierre's Hole, as well as the sources of the Snake River. But perhaps most important of all, John Colter was the first to pass through the breathtaking region that has since become Yellowstone National Park. Lastly, he saw the immense tar spring at the fork of the Stinkingwater (Shoshone) River. This spot came to be known as "Colter's Hell," and it is the adventure that took place here for which John Colter is best remembered.

Manuel Lisa sent Colter back into the mountains to visit the Blackfeet, apparently thinking he could smooth over any harsh feelings the Indians might have toward him. With him was his old friend, Potts, one of the men who had originally lured him into the fur trade. At a branch of the Missouri River called Jefferson's Fork, Colter and Potts were checking their traps when they were suddenly surrounded by several hundred Blackfeet. According to Colter, Potts, in a fit of madness, took a shot at one of the Blackfeet and was soon "made a riddle of."

The Indians then seized Colter, stripping the man naked. After discussing what would be done with their prisoner, the tribe decided that they would run Colter down. Still naked, Colter was taken three or four hundred yards out in front of the tribe and told to run for his life. And John Colter did just that, running barefoot over a prairie filled with prickly pears. At one point in the chase, a brave came within twenty yards of Colter and threw his lance, missing him. Colter quickly picked up the lance and killed the young brave before continuing his flight.

Throughout the day the sun burned his skin, and his feet ached and bled until they were beyond recognition. He was hungry but had no time to stop to eat. And by his own estimate, he was at least seven days from Fort Lisa, the nearest post. Depite the incredible odds against him, John Colter's mountaineering skills enabled him to survive. He hid in rivers, continually escaping the clutches of his pursuers. His only food was a root favored by the Indians of the area, and it kept him alive. Seven days later, half dead, he arrived at Fort Lisa.

In the spring of 1810, Colter finally made his way back to St. Louis. It was here that he gave important data to William Clark, who was working on the map he had drawn during the voyage of exploration. Colter had many tales to tell, but some of the things he saw seemed too unbelievable to be true. Like many mountain men, he was branded a liar rather than a credible storyteller.

John Colter was the first white explorer to pass though the Rocky Mountains, with their breathtaking vistas and bubbling hot springs.

In December of 1813, John Colter died of jaundice in St. Louis. Sadly, it would be at least a dozen years before another mountain man, Jim Bridger, would take in the sights that Colter had seen in his years in the Rockies.

With the opening of the West in the early nineteenth century, many young men pursued their fortune in the fur trade.

CHAPTER II
MANUEL LISA
(1772 – 1820)

By the time he was twenty, Manuel Lisa had become an active fur trader in New Orleans, the city of his birth. He was one of the leading traders of the century, and in 1802 the Spanish government granted him a monopoly for trade with the Osage Indians.

After 1807 Lisa averaged about one expedition a year. During his first expedition, in 1807, he established a trading post at the mouth of the Big Horn River, in what is now Montana. The following spring, he built a fort there, which he at first named after his son Raymond, but later called Fort Manuel. This was the first such outpost in the Upper Missouri River country, an area of prairies and rolling hills on the Great Plains.

Since the Louisiana Purchase of 1803 and the success of the Lewis and Clark expedition, St. Louis had become the crossroads of western expansion as well

Spaniard Manuel Lisa led several trapping expeditions up the Missouri River, and his establishment of a trading post at Fort Lisa was important to the growing traffic in furs.

as the starting point for many exploring and trading parties. Consequently, in 1809 Lisa worked with the famous explorer William Clark, as well as Jean-Pierre Chouteau, Andrew Henry, and others to form the St. Louis Missouri Fur Company. The company sent out its first expedition of 350 men in 1809, and continued to outfit prosperous missions until 1814.

Of Lisa's twelve to fourteen expeditions up the Missouri River, the most famous was in 1811. Setting out in a river barge, at the head of a search party, Lisa overtook boats that had been sent by another fur magnate, John Jacob Astor, three weeks earlier. The race became legendary among rivermen.

In 1812 the Spaniard built Fort Lisa near the site of present-day Omaha, Nebraska. For a decade this was the most important post on the Upper Missouri.

In 1814 Lisa married a woman of the Omaha tribe (his second of three marriages). That same year he was appointed sub-agent for the Indian tribes on the Missouri above the mouth of the Kansas River by William Clark, by then governor of Missouri Territory. He spent his last winter at Fort Lisa with his third wife and died in St. Louis on August 12, 1820.

For a man who accomplished as much as he did, Manuel Lisa was not particularly liked by his men. Still, he accomplished quite a bit in his time, and not all of his achievements were connected with trapping and the fur trade. For example, he proved invaluable to the United States government during the War of 1812 by maintaining peaceful and friendly relations with the western Indian tribes. And the exploratory work of his men—John Colter and George Drouillard, in particular—was instrumental in providing geographical knowledge of a great deal of the Northwest Territory.

The Blackfoot Indians were very peaceful toward white fur traders at first, but as relations turned sour, they became a constant threat to mountain men.

St. Louis served as a starting point for several trapping expeditions.

But most of all, Manuel Lisa will be remembered as a premier fur trader. He laid down the principles for successful trading operations on the Upper Missouri River. Although his many expeditions never actually took him into the mountain areas of the West, he was responsible for keeping the river traffic open to them, for he knew that in the mountains the real profits in the fur trade would be made. These profits would be made by men who were free to trap the bountiful streams of the Rockies, and who would bring their pelts to a rendezvous point each year and be resupplied by St. Louis.

In addition to his exploits as a fur trader, Jedediah
Strong Smith made many important explorations
of areas such as the Mojave Desert and the
Sacramento Basin in California.

CHAPTER III

JEDEDIAH STRONG SMITH

(1799 – 1831)

Jedediah Smith was anything but the typical mountain man. One of the few New Englanders who ventured into the fur trade, Smith was a clean-shaven and religious young man, attributes seldom seen among his counterparts in the business. But perhaps more significant was the fact that he seemed to have a keener sense of the importance of exploration than many of his fellow mountain men. And because of this

Many mountain men took great risks when hunting
big game, such as encountering grizzly bears.

strong desire to chart the wilderness, Smith will be remembered for his achievements as a great explorer as well as for his exploits as a trapper.

Little is known of Smith's early years other than the fact that he received a basic elementary education before going to work in the Lake Erie trade.

In 1822, he showed up in St. Louis, at about the same time William Ashley and Andrew Henry advertised for "100 enterprising young men" who would be willing to join a fur-trading expedition into the West for a period of two to three years. His first journey up the Missouri River, in June of 1822, was part of what became known as the Ashley-Henry Expedition. The expedition effectively brought under American control the vast territory outside of the Oregon country, which was previously dominated by the English.

In 1823, he ascended the Missouri again with the Ashley-Henry party, and he proved to be one of the most courageous men ever to live in the mountains. In September of that year, somewhere west of the Black Hills, Smith was fearfully mauled by a grizzly bear, barely managing to escape death. The bear had torn off a portion of scalp on the left side of his head, and almost completely tore off the young leader's left ear, leaving it to hang from his head by a mere thread. As calm as could be, Smith sat down and asked his friend and fellow mountain man, James Clyman, to get the sewing kit from his bag and sew the ear back on. Back then there were no painkillers like those we have today. But to the astonishment of Clyman and the others in the group, Jed Smith didn't utter one word in pain from the time the grizzly bear had attacked him until Clyman had totally sewed the ear back in place.

It was early the next year, 1824, with Tom Fitzpatrick, that Smith rediscovered the South Pass, a major gateway to the Northwest in what is now the state of Wyoming. In 1812, South Pass had been discovered from the west side by Robert Stuart, an employee of John Jacob Astor. Smith's party discovered it from the east side, and has since been credited with the discovery of the South Pass.

In 1826, Smith and two partners, David E. Jackson and William L. Sublette, bought out Ashley's interests and formed a trading company at Great Salt Lake, Utah. That year he led an expedition from Great Salt Lake across the deserts of southern California. From San Gabriel he journeyed northward to the American River (just east of Sacramento), and in May 1827, on his return to Great Salt Lake, he crossed the Sierra Nevada and the deserts of the Great Basin, becoming the first white man to follow that route. Later in the year he retraced his path to San Gabriel, survived an attack by Mojave Indians (although ten of his men did not), and went up to the Sacramento Valley. The following spring, contrary to the wishes of the Mexican government, he continued northwest, then north along the coast to Fort Vancouver, on the Columbia River in Oregon. His travels opened up the coastal route to that territory, where he remained until the spring of 1829.

In 1830, he and his partners sold their fur-trading interests to a new company that had been organized by Jim Bridger, Tom Fitzpatrick, Milton Sublette (William's brother), and others, and in 1831 he joined the Santa Fe trade.

Smith was killed by Comanche Indians on the Cimarron River on May 27, 1831, en route to Santa Fe. Without a doubt, his explorations were surpassed in importance only by those of Lewis and Clark. But his geographical discoveries were only passed on orally among other mountain men, and his maps were published in obscure works. Thus, his accomplishments remained virtually unknown for years. But as westward migration increased, Smith's achievements became more widely known. He is now considered to be the first American explorer to enter California from the east, the

Together with Tom Fitzpatrick, Jedediah Smith
discovered the South Pass, a major gateway to the
Northwest, in present-day Wyoming.

first to explore the land of the northern California-Oregon coast, and the first to cross the Sierra Nevada from west to east.

Jedediah Smith was all business, perhaps lacking a sense of humor, and could be impatient with delays or distractions. As great an explorer and trapper as he was, Smith's chief weakness was his inability to forge friendlier relations with American Indians. In addition to his ten men killed by Mojave Indians, fourteen more were massacred by Umpqua Indians along the Oregon coast in 1828. On many occasions, his strong religious faith and devotion to family had sustained Smith through desert thirst, mountain hardships, and American Indian hostility until he finally fell before Comanche warriors. Though he was highly respected by his peers, Jedediah Smith was a man who stood alone. And for better or for worse, he died that way, too.

Although he was known for his tall tales, mountain
man Jim Bridger was respected as a guide
and scout.

CHAPTER IV
JIM BRIDGER
(1804 – 1881)

For a man as knowledgeable about the frontier west of the Rockies as he was, Jim Bridger was shockingly illiterate, even by the standards of the mountain men. A few years after Bridger's birth in Richmond, Virginia, both his parents died, and as a result, he never received even the most basic education. He was apprenticed to a blacksmith until 1822, when he responded to a newspaper advertisement, and joined William H. Ashley and Andrew Henry on their first fur-trapping expedition from St. Louis to the headwaters of the Missouri River. For the next twenty years he remained in the West as a trapper, gaining an incomparable knowledge of the country and becoming one of the most famous mountain men.

If young Bridger ever had anything to be ashamed of, it was most likely an incident that took place on that first trip west with Ashley and Henry. One of the older mountain men, a man by the name of Hugh Glass, got into a losing fight with a grizzly bear, not unlike the encounter Jed Smith had had with one that same year. Unfortunately, Hugh Glass was mauled even worse than Smith, and appeared to be near death. The rest of the group moved on, leaving young Bridger and another man to watch over Glass's body until he died. Perhaps it was because of the American Indian activity in the area, no one is certain, but Bridger and his partner abandoned the mutilated body of Glass, believing he could never live. Hugh Glass did survive, however, and finally caught up with Bridger some 350 miles away at Fort Kiowa. To his credit, Glass forgave Bridger the gross error he had made.

Young Bridger appears more positively in history when, in 1824, he became the first white man to see the Great Salt Lake, at first believing the body of extremely salty water to be an arm of the Pacific Ocean. It isn't known if he was the only one to make this discovery, but he is the only one to have given an eyewitness account of this finding. It was also the report of this discovery that put him in league with John Colter, for like Colter, few people would believe his story. Thus,

Since Jim Bridger's discovery of the Great Salt Lake in 1824, the site has become a tourist attraction. The lake presently contains about 6,000,000,000 tons of mineral salt.

Jim Bridger obtained a reputation as one of the best and biggest "liars" in the West, a reputation he sometimes deserved, but not in this case.

In 1830 he formed a partnership with Thomas Fitzpatrick, Milton Sublette, and others, and bought out the former Ashley interests that had been held by Jed Smith

Jim Bridger established Fort Bridger in Wyoming, which served as an important starting point for surveying expeditions.

for four years. This new organization was called the Rocky Mountain Fur Company, and it dominated the western fur trade until 1834.

In 1832 Bridger and his partners ventured into hostile American Indian country for furs, and in one skirmish the big mountain man received an arrow in his back. For one reason or another the arrow was not removed until three years later, when Dr. Marcus Whitman stopped at the 1835 Green River Rendezvous and operated on Bridger's back. Bridger was a rather outspoken man, and so when Dr. Whitman marveled at the fact that the mountain man was still alive after three years with an arrow in his back, Bridger simply snarled to the doctor, "Meat don't spoil in the Rockies."

Although the fur trade was on the decline, Bridger established Fort Bridger on the Oregon Trail in Wyoming in 1843. During the following ten years, he served as scout and guide for a number of exploring and surveying expeditions.

Around 1849 he discovered Bridger's Pass in southern Wyoming. In 1853 he was driven from the region by the recently arrived Mormons, and retired for a time to a farm near Kansas City, Missouri. But four years later he returned to the West as a guide in the army campaign against the Mormons.

A man gifted with a keen memory, Bridger came as close as he ever would to being a literate man during the early 1860s. Fascinated by the story of Hiawatha, read to him by an army captain, the mountain man inquired as to who the greatest writer was. The captain replied, "Shakespeare." Bridger then traveled up and down the Oregon Trail until he found someone who had a complete set of Shakespeare's works. He traded a yoke of cattle for the playwright's volumes and hired a German boy for forty dollars a month to read to him. He would then wander through the camp, quoting Shakespeare, adding a few of his own oaths to liven up the story lines. Asked which of the great poet's plays he liked best, Bridger said it was *King Lear,* although he confessed that Lear did remind him of his own brother-in-law, an American Indian, who he thought was mean.

From 1865 to 1866, he worked as a guide and explorer in the building of the Powder River army road that followed the route of the Bozeman Trail.

He remained in the West, fabled as the "Old Man of the Mountains," until 1868, when he once again retired to his farm. During the last years of his life his eyesight failed him, and he eventually went blind. But he was never short of stories about his days as a mountain man. He died on that farm on July 17, 1881.

Many emigrants
and prospecters
found their way to the West by the Oregon Trail,
which was mapped by the hardy, enterprising
mountain men. To this day, ruts in the earth mark
the ground where wagon wheels once rode.

James Beckwourth was one of the few African-Americans to venture out to the West in search of a fortune. During his lifetime, his taste for adventure took him to the Rockies, Florida, and the gold camps of California.

CHAPTER V
JAMES P. BECKWOURTH
(1798 – 1866)

Of all the trappers and traders who explored the Far West, Jim Beckwourth had to be one of the most interesting. He was born in Virginia, the son of Sir Jennings Beckwith and a slave woman of mixed race. Though he was legally born a slave, Beckwourth was regarded by his earliest employers as a free black man, indicating that he had been freed by his father. Thereafter, he was able to move about as he pleased. When he turned fourteen he was apprenticed to a blacksmith in St. Louis, where he would spend the next five years.

Beckwourth didn't join the original band of "enterprising young men" in 1823, as did Smith and Bridger. Instead, he waited until the fall of 1824, when he joined General William Ashley's third expedition into the Rockies. This expedition would lead to the famous fur-trading rendezvous that took place on the Green River, starting in the summer of 1825.

Beckwourth wintered in Cache Valley from 1825 to 1826 and served heroically in the "fight in the willows" between the Blackfoot tribe and Robert Campbell's group of trappers, who had been attacked on their way to a rendezvous in 1828. According to Beckwourth, he saved his party from disaster by charging through Indian lines and contacting a rescue outfit.

With the end of the Rendezvous of 1828, Beckwourth stopped trapping with Smith, Jackson, and Sublette until early 1829, when he signed a promissory note to settle his debts with these men. It was at this time, when he was with Robert Campbell, that he took an interest in, and became involved with, the Crow Indians, who were relatively peaceful toward the mountain men. The first five years he spent with the tribe were more of an initiation than anything else, for it was during this period that he learned to speak the Crow language and adopted the customs and habits of the tribe. Beckwourth wasn't the first explorer to be accepted into an American Indian tribe, nor would he be the last. As long as he could pick up the ways of the tribe and show himself to be a good warrior, so much the better. If Beckwourth was indeed a "chief" of the Crow, as he claimed, it was because he would eagerly participate in the raids they made on their enemies, particularly the Blackfoot Indians. Although Beckwourth tended to exaggerate when describing his life with the Crow Indians, he definitely furnished his readers with an accurate depiction of what life with the Crow was like.

During the summer of 1835, Beckwourth and a vagabond named Thomas "Peg Leg" Smith took up horse stealing in California. Although this "profession" did earn him a tidy profit, he soon gave it up for other prospects.

Beckwourth next appeared in Florida as a muleteer to fight the Seminole Indians in the Seminole War. He worked briefly as a trader on the Santa Fe Trail. Then, in 1842, with several other independent traders, he moved to the Arkansas River and built a small fort on Fountain Creek, which they called "Pueblo."

For more than six years, James Beckwourth lived among the Crow Indians.

Never one to settle down, Beckwourth was off to California two years later. When the Mexican War began in 1846, General Stephen W. Kearny led the U.S. Army to California, where they took control. According to Beckwourth, the general asked him to serve as a messenger between Santa Fe and Fort Leavenworth.

It wasn't until 1851 that Jim Beckwourth took part in the Gold Rush of California. However, instead of panning for gold, like most who ventured there, he hit upon a different way to make his fortune. During his exploration of the Sierras between the Feather River and Truckee River, he found an excellent wagon road that would easily transport the many emigrants flocking to northern California. While others interested in this project began to raise money, Beckwourth set out to attract emigrants willing to give his route a try. On August 31, 1851, the first wagon to travel through what would become known as Beckwourth Pass reached Marysville.

It was in the spring of 1854, at Indian Bar, that Jim Beckwourth first met Thomas D. Bonner. It seemed Bonner had been a newspaperman before the Gold Rush. Like many during the Gold Rush days, Bonner was open to any money-making proposition, and readily accepted Beckwourth's proposal to write the mountain man's memoirs. In 1856, *The Life and Adventures of James P. Beckwourth, Mountaineer, Scout, Pioneer and Chief of the Crow Nation,* by Thomas Daniel Bonner, was published. If it hadn't been for Bonner, the mountain man's name would never have been changed from "Beckwith" to the more presently accepted "Beckwourth."

Once again it was the discovery of gold that put Jim Beckwourth on the move. This time, it was the 1859 gold strike in the Pikes Peak area of the Kansas Territory that drew him. When he arrived in Denver, Beckwourth's old friend Louis Vasquez hired him on as a supplier and storekeeper.

Perhaps one of his darkest days was when he joined the Third Regiment of the Colorado Volunteer Cavalry, probably as a guide and interpreter. It was Colonel John M. Chivington and his "Bloodless Third" that were to blame for the notorious attack on the Cheyenne camp at Sand Creek on November 29, 1864. Whether or not Beckwourth actually took part in the Sand Creek Massacre is arguable. Feeling the way he did about American Indians, it is highly doubtful that he took part in this slaughter.

Apparently, Beckwourth died on a hunting trip in 1866. Others believe he died not far from Denver in 1867. Sources vary. How he died is just as controversial as the date of his death. Depending on your reference, Beckwourth was either poisoned by the Crow, who believed he had brought smallpox to the tribe in 1837, or he became sick on a visit to the Crow and died a natural death.

Like John Colter and Jim Bridger, Beckwourth was known to tell his share of tall tales and thus gained the label of "gaudy liar." However, from the legacy of his forty years on the frontier (1825–1865), we get a glimpse of what a fur trapper's life with American Indians was like. But perhaps more important, we also witness the experiences of an African-American mountain man.

An immigrant from Ireland, Tom "Broken Hand" Fitzpatrick made his way to the West, where he became a fur trader, and eventually a skillful Indian agent.

CHAPTER VI
TOM "BROKEN HAND" FITZPATRICK
(1799 – 1854)

Born about 1799 in County Cavan, Ireland, Tom Fitzpatrick emigrated to the United States about 1816 and made his way to the frontier. During the years he lived in America, he would hold careers as a mountain man, guide, and Indian agent.

After spending a brief period trading with the Indians, he joined William H. Ashley and

Andrew Henry on their second trapping expedition to the Rocky Mountains in 1823.

It was Fitzpatrick who accompanied Jed Smith in the explorations that led to the discovery of South Pass through the Rockies in 1824.

For several years he remained in the mountains as a trapper, and in 1830 he joined Jim Bridger, Milton Sublette, and others in organizing the Rocky Mountain Fur Company. Fitzpatrick was acknowledged as the head of the company. The Rocky Mountain Fur Company dominated the fur trade until John Jacob Astor's American Fur Company appeared in the region. By 1834 the competition and dwindling trade forced the partners to disband. By that time Fitzpatrick was reputed by his peers to be the greatest of the mountain men. Despite the breakup of his company, he worked for Astor for a time.

In 1832 Fitzpatrick earned one of several nicknames that would stick with him through the years. Pursued by a band of Gros Ventres, he lost his horse, rifle, and equipment as he made his escape. Lacking food, he eventually collapsed, but fortunately was found by a group of searchers from a rendezvous party who had been sent to look for him. He was hardly recognizable, for the experience had turned his hair gray. Although he recovered, he was often called "White Hair" by comrades and American Indians.

The second nickname also had to do with being pursued by American Indians, this time the Blackfoot Indians. In 1835, a band of hostile warriors chased him to the edge of a cliff. Knowing it was certain death to be caught by Blackfeet, Fitzpatrick spurred his horse and jumped off the cliff, falling forty feet into a river and, miraculously, surviving to swim across it. On the far side of the river, Fitzpatrick was pulling the cover off his rifle when, somehow, his rifle discharged, shattering his left wrist. The mountain man survived the accident but was known from then on—particularly by American Indians—as "Broken Hand."

Occasionally he worked as a guide, and in 1841 he led the California-bound emigrant wagon train of John Bartleson and John Bidwell as far as Fort Hall. Fitzpatrick then conducted part of the group, including Father Pierre Jean De Smet, to the Oregon country.

From 1843 to 1844 he worked with Kit Carson, a guide for one of Captain John C. Fremont's expeditions, and in 1845 he guided Colonel Stephen W. Kearny's exploration of the South Pass. The next year he led Kearny to Santa Fe and on toward California.

That year he was appointed Indian agent for the Upper Platte region, with responsibility for dealing with the Cheyenne, the Arapaho, and some Sioux bands. Long respected and sometimes feared by American Indians of the northern plains, in September 1851

Several disputes with American Indians were resolved by the U.S. Indian Peace Commission. Many mountain men were chosen for the commission because of their years of experience in dealing with various tribes.

Fitzpatrick called a great council of chiefs at Fort Laramie, persuading them, by gifts and argument, to accept the notion of occupying lands reserved for the various tribes, with each area clearly demarked and guaranteed. The Sioux, Mandan, Gros Ventres, Assiniboin, Crow, Blackfoot, Cheyenne, and Arapaho Indians were present, and all accepted the treaty that, unknown to them, was destined to make it still easier for the lands of any tribe to be taken by white men, and that would lead directly to Indian wars in the decades to come. In 1853 Fitzpatrick negotiated another settlement with the Comanche and Kiowa at Fort Atkinson, near the site of present-day Dodge City, Kansas.

He was then called to Washington, D.C., to discuss Indian affairs, but died of pneumonia in a hotel soon after arriving, on February 7, 1854. He was buried in the Congressional Cemetery.

Tom Fitzpatrick was an outstanding mountain man and was highly respected as both a guide and an Indian agent. After his death, Chief Black Kettle of the Cheyenne said: "Major Fitzpatrick was a good man. He told us that when he was gone, we would have trouble, and it has proved true."

As a fur trapper,
Kit Carson journeyed
as far west as New
Mexico, and as far
north as Montana.

CHAPTER VII
CHRISTOPHER "KIT" CARSON
(1809 – 1868)

Of all the men of the "mountain man era," perhaps Kit Carson is best remembered. After looking at the man's life and the feats he accomplished, it is easy to understand why.

Born in Madison County, Kentucky, Christopher Carson spent his early childhood in Boone's Lick, on the Missouri frontier. He received no formal schooling, and in 1825 was apprenticed to a saddle maker, but ran away to join an expedition to Santa Fe. Under the guidance of Ewing Young, he learned to trap for furs and fight Indians, and established a home base in the region of Taos, New Mexico. Carson trapped in California and as far north as Montana, at various times associating with Tom Fitzpatrick, Jim Bridger, and other famous mountain men.

During the 1840s, Kit Carson joined the U.S. Army and distinguished himself as a hero during the Mexican War. Eventually he became a U.S. Indian agent to the Utes.

It was at the Rendezvous of 1835 that Kit Carson accomplished something that would pass into legend. Both he and a big Frenchman named Shunar had taken a liking to a young girl from the Arapaho tribe. At one point Carson told the bully to shut up "or he would rip his guts." Both men went for a gun, mounted their horses, and rode directly toward each other at a fierce gallop. Shunar fired his rifle, just grazing Carson's head and neck. At the same time, Carson fired a pistol, wounding the man in the shoulder. When Carson went for another pistol, the big Frenchman, suddenly not so tough, begged for his life. Carson married the Arapaho girl not long afterward.

On a steamboat from St. Louis, Carson met John C. Fremont, who later engaged him as a guide on three expeditions during the 1840s. He took part in several battles for the conquest of California and later, while visiting Washington, discovered that his exploits with Fremont and his daring in the war had made him a national hero.

In 1853 Carson was appointed U.S. Indian agent to the Ute tribe. Even though he was illiterate, he was extremely effective in that position. Kit did what he could to try to make the Indian's life a better one, and because of this, he was greatly respected by the Utes.

John C. Fremont's daring campaigns during the Mexican War secured a lot of new territory for the United States.

He dictated his government reports to other people. One of his scribes, an army surgeon named Peters, took down his autobiography, but embellished it so much that Carson later said he thought Dr. Peters "had laid it on a leetle too thick."

Carson resigned as an Indian agent when the Civil War began in 1861. He was given the rank of colonel, and raised a volunteer regiment, the First New Mexico Volunteer Infantry. While the Union forces east of the Mississippi fought the Confederates, Carson successfully battled American Indian tribes that had fought settlers in the Southwest for years. But his final battle in Texas, the Battle of Adobe Walls, in 1864, was a defeat. Five thousand Indians met his poorly armed group of 400 soldiers, and retreat was inevitable. Nevertheless, he was made brigadier general of volunteers, and in 1866 he was named commander of Fort Garland, Colorado, but had to resign the next year due to poor health.

Although his health continued to decline, he attended a conference in Washington with the Utes, and made a fruitless trip to the East, hoping to find medical relief. On May 23, 1868, he died at Fort Lyon, Colorado.

Kit Carson wasn't a very imposing man; he was only five foot six inches tall. And like Jed Smith, he went against the stereotype we have of mountain men, being clean shaven and soft spoken. He was temperate, modest, and widely respected. He was not only a mountain man, but a guide, an Indian agent, and a soldier. Of all the famous men of his time—Smith, Bridger, and Fitzpatrick, for example—Kit Carson was the only one to achieve the status of national hero during his lifetime.

Whether or not they have become household names, all the mountain men are national heroes. The nation today is secure in its boundaries, the vast span of the continent charted from coast to coast. We owe this comfort to the mountain men. Although the wilds of the West may seem tame now, in the days of the mountain men they were as remote and forbidding as outer space.

For Further Reading

Allen, John Logan. *Jedediah Smith and the Mountain Men of the American West*. New York: Chelsea House Publishers, 1991.

Blassingame, Wyatt. *Jim Beckwourth: Black Trapper and Indian Chief*. New York: Chelsea Juniors, 1991.

Christian, Mary Blount. *Who'd Believe John Colter?* New York: Macmillan Publishing Company, 1993.

Fitz-Gerald, Christine Maloney. *Meriwether Lewis and William Clark*. Chicago: Children's Press, 1991.

Harris, Edward D. *John Charles Fremont and the Great Western Reconnaissance*. New York: Chelsea House Publishers, 1990.

Miller, Brandon Marie. *Buffalo Gals: Women of the Old West*. Minneapolis, MN: Lerner Publications, 1995.

Press, Petra. *A Multicultural Portrait of the Move West*. New York: Marshall Cavendish Corporation, 1993.

Sandler, Martin W. *Pioneers: A Library of Congress Book*. New York: HarperCollins, 1994.

Index

ABOUT THE AUTHOR

James L. Collins is the author of a number of books for Frankin Watts on the American West. In addition to writing nonfiction for young people he is also a prolific author of Western novels. He lives in Fort Collins, Colorado.